# Emotions Beyond Words

Trupti Kotbagi

BookLeaf Publishing

India | USA | UK

Presentation by *BookLeaf Publishing*

Web: www.bookleafpub.com

E-mail: info@bookleafpub.com

ISBN: 9789358369359

First edition 2023

# DEDICATION

I dedicate this book to the Journey of Life I have tread so far. I wish to extend my dedication to every person I have met in life who has contributed to every emotion I have felt at different stages in my life.

# ACKNOWLEDGEMENT

I want to acknowledge my deepest gratitude to BookLeaf Publishing for giving a chance to rookies like me to get out of their comfort zones and try something different. BookLeaf has given me an opportunity to do something I had never dreamt of.

# PREFACE

Do First, Ask Forgiveness Later; literally, because this is my first shot at writing poems, and it sure has a huge room for improvement ;)
This is an attempt at doing something which I had never imagined doing before.
We go through a lot, but it is hard to put even basic emotions into words.
At times, we want to express how overwhelming emotions get, but struggle to find the right words and means to express them. Writing has proved to be a strong weapon for silent warriors of emotions. Poems are my refuge to let out the storm of strong emotions and feelings buried deep within.
Hopefully, the readers will find this collection of raw poems written by me a bit relatable. I request you all to keep your minds and hearts open to accept this honest effort in poetry.

# Alone Not Lonely

Just be by yourself.
Even if you have no one
Just be by yourself.
Smile when the lips smile,
Cry when the eyes cry.
Take control of your tears
Feel the power in your smile
And take charge of every emotion you feel.
Keep an open heart to let them go who are
meant to leave,
Close your arms and keep who are meant to stay.
You will feel the warm hug of that person you
have known since your birth, YOU.
You are alone, not lonely
Just let go of the fears of being by yourself.


-        PoeTiK

# Perfect Love

To hug you once,
And treasure the feel of your
touch forever,
And never let anyone get
close to you ever again.
Not to live in the refuge of your love,
But to own the love that was never mine.
The memory of which, makes my eyes twinkle
and face glow,
How my love is still perfect, even without
having you.


- PoeTiK

# Mismatch

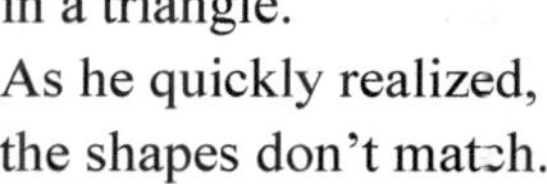

At daycare one day,
caught my eye a sight,
A toddler trying to
match shapes – a square
in a triangle.
As he quickly realized,
the shapes don't match.
Happily, he accepted the mismatch and
continued playing.
I smiled and thought, how simple it is;
Accepting the differences, and not imposing the
need to match.
To match the material and match the abstract;
To match the tangible and the intangible;
Why can the world not normalize mismatches by
embracing the differences?
To opening our minds and hearts towards
acceptance, that Mismatch is uniquely normal.


\-       PoeTiK

# Quit Quitting

One day, with
misty eyes, I
dialed my mom
"Mom, I cannot
do this anymore.
I don't see it getting easy anymore,
I have lost the battle, I am giving up".
"Can I speak to my daughter?", were the words
from the other side,
"My daughter never gives up!"
She continued – "I have lost a lot in life, lost
enough, for you and for me
You were born with a purpose, a purpose to fight
and to win
I have and will lose whatever possible to let you
keep winning.
One thing you continue doing is to 'STOP
QUITTNG'"
It was that day and it is today,
I kept treading along, with the legacy of fighting
spirit I received from my mother.


-          PoeTiK

# Life is
# Beautiful

My love, life is
beautiful.
Seeing you till the eyes
are full, is beautiful.
Your voice from across
the lake,
When travels to me
with the breeze, is
beautiful.
In the fragrance of wet soil, in the deep breath of
the wind,
When the trees soak themselves, is beautiful.
The scents of flowers fade away, the give and
take of breath goes away,
Being is beautiful and going away is beautiful.
My Love, life is beautiful!

\-     PoeTiK

# Unsaid

I often remember
those things,
Which remained
unsaid to you.
I have carefully
saved the letters,
Which were left
unsent to you.
I have lived all those moments till now,
I longed to live with you.
There is love still in my heart,
Which stays unexpressed to you.
I still remember hearing everything,
That was never expressed by you.
Wish the unsaid is said one day, some day...

-        PoeTiK

# I Am Love

I am not a script written
on the shore, which is
erased by the waves,
I am not a raindrop that
stops after raining,
Nor am I a dream that
fades from the memory.
I am not a gust of wind
that comes and goes,
And not the moon that
sets after night.

I am that feeling, which merges in you and flows
in your blood,
I am that color, In your heart, that will never
come off.
I am those lyrics of that song which your lips
will sing forever,
I am the fire that will burn itself to lighten the
world,
A dream, the wind, and a candle that spread
light,
Which will exist forever,
This forever feeling is love, I am Love.


\-         PoeTiK

# Why??

At the bottom of a
numb heart,
Can you tell what's
hidden?
The throbbing pain
in the heart,
Can the body
unravel?
Why the never-ending game of waves and tides
Can the ocean discover?
From the bane of the new moon night,
Why do we long to free the moon?
To the magical laugh of blooming flowers,
Can nature leash the shrink?
What's the real meaning of being alive,
Can we uncover?
Journey of life is a rocky road,
Can someone tell if death is easy?
In search of my soul,
Can I find myself?
In the loss of all consciousness,
Can I revive the purpose of life?


-      PoeTiK

# My Life

You are the relief in my
wait,
You are the desire of my
heart,
The world is because
you are,
I look for words to
express what you mean
to me.
Pardon my effort to
speak my heart out;
To tell you what you mean to me.
You are the blessing I asked for,
You are the light who lits up my world,
You are the evening breeze of refreshing
fragrance.
You are the glass of never-ending love,
You are just another name of my life.
You are that breath of my fading life,
You are the only, you are my life.

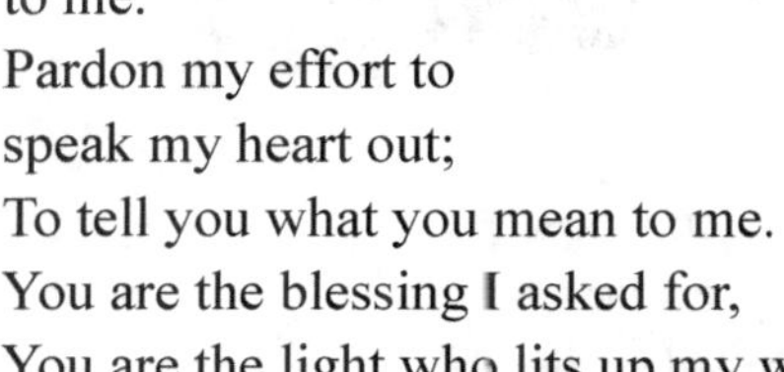

-      PoeTiK

# Journey To The Destination

How strange that
night was,
Had its own
charming story.
Life had her plans
when we just sat
dreaming…
Learned about the
world a little,
and set a
destination.

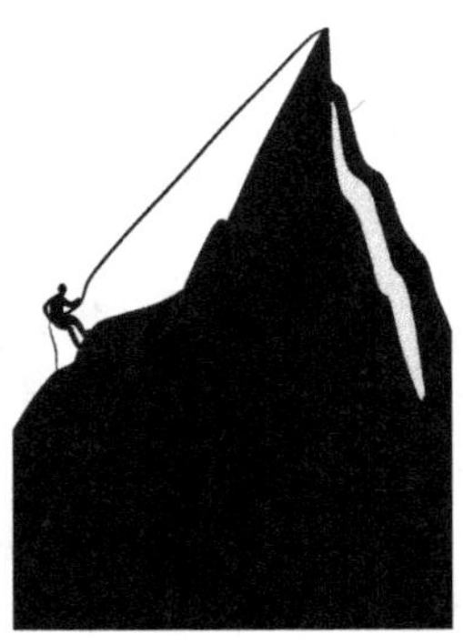

Let go of some memories,
Forgot all false promises.
The sky then bowed its head,
And the sea paved the way.
Fought with hell when Mother Earth supported,
Befriended the light and fought the dark,
Gathered our breath, to twist and turn our life.
Collected all the stones in our way,
Made them the gems in the journey to the
destination.

-       PoeTiK

# That Someone

If there is someone
who listens, just listen
to my eyes,
Because I often lock
my lips and carry
stories in my eyes.
He came to talk and
instead made eye
contact with me,
I heard what you didn't want to say
And my heart broke into pieces.
Broke every corner of the heart and shattered
every wall
Should there be someone keen on peeping in,
and staying back?
Because the heart is a house full of damages, not
asking for repairs
Just craving for the company of that person who
enters its broken walls and tells it aloud that
some of the dirty walls can still be painted.
Some pictures are still old, can be thrown away
By the way, a lot of damage has been done due
but its foundation is still safe.

There should be someone who just looks at me
and tells me that this smile is beautiful but not
special
Special is this wound that you have earned and
not worn
Tell me that what I see is unreal
Tell me that I keep my poems as a veil in front
of my mind, see through the curtain.
Tell me that my smiles are just my failed
attempts to curb your passion
Tell me to take off this mask and look in the
mirror to see myself, and not to hide
Tell me that you are the face of pain, cracked,
worn
And the pain that is beautiful
There is love, tell me, you are the pain, you are
beautiful, you are love


-       PoeTiK

# Eye To An Eye

That eye to an eye is so
dope, gets to me like a
wine
That eye of the world is
also evil, so should I
just whine
My eyes wait for those
eyes, wonder what
should I name them
That look keeps
expressing love, should
I name it rose
That eye to an eye is like a wave, floods my
heart with emotions
I can read through that look, that I want to write
a book
How many eyes have they met, there is no
account of it, I bet
How many questions have those eyes asked me;
I look for the answers to be..


\-        PoeTiK

# Right And Wrong

Who gets to judge what is
right and what is not?
What I wear today is right
for some and wrong for
others,
For some I am
dark-skinned, for others I
am dark in character!
This is right and that is
wrong,
Ever wondered, what is in
between right and wrong?
When it is right why is it right and if it is wrong
why is it so?
Why sometimes the right feels wrong and the
other way round?
Just want to know who gets to make this
decision.
Is it right to think of others while embracing
someone?
The one you embrace is not right, then how is
the one in your thoughts right?
If your heart constantly longs for the forbidden
one

Would it be wrong to turn a blind eye, when he
suddenly appears in front?
And if this is wrong then when it is right
Who decides, this is right and that is wrong?
If loving him from the bottom of my heart is
right
Then why do I feel it wrong if he loves someone
else?
If he is right then why am I considered wrong?
If hurting someone physically is punishable,
Then hurting someone's feelings, shouldn't that
be punishable?
Who decides, this is right and that is wrong?


-      PoeTiK

# Old friends, New Times

Let me go knock on
the doors of some
old friends
Let's see if their
wings are tired or
are they still
flapping
Let's see if they laugh out loud or just smile with
their lips closed
Let's see if they narrate everything about their
journey or just brag about success stories.
Will they have a big smile on their faces, seeing
me or will they look at the clock indicating the
time for me to leave?
Let me go knock on the doors of some old
friends.


-       PoeTiK

# Fall In Love Again

Fell in love for the
first time, or did I just
feel that was love
I realized that some
people come into life
just to make us
realize
What we do not want
from love
I do not want someone who thinks he owns me
I do not want someone who knows you only by
your body
I do not want the one whose world revolves
around himself
I do not want someone who loves the
manipulated morph of me
I do not want someone who leashes me like a
puppet
Not someone who brings pain to me, even after
pouring torrents of love
Pain is the fate of love, they say.
Have had enough, just let go, says the grieved
mind.
The heart however craves another chance.
It knows, it's not fine although it seems fine.

Shouting it out, the mind says you have
everything you need.
Oh dear heart, tell me what you need.
The mind has sensed the lies, the pain of love
that ends before the time,
That's why this time, the mind shuts the doors
tight.
The mind is full of anguish, until you fall out of
love.
Oh my heart, let go off! This love is beyond
your understanding.
Oh wait, but, what is love if you understand it.
The heart learns this bitter but beautiful truth,
I am ready to fall in love again!


-       PoeTiK

# You Are Beautiful

You are beautiful,
tell this to
yourself a
hundred times,
While walking,
stopping, sitting,
standing,
sleeping, waking,
smiling, crying,
When looking at

yourself in the mirror, say "You are beautiful".
When gazing into someone's eyes and catching
your own reflection,
Carefree of what he is thinking about you,
Feel free to tell yourself, "You are beautiful".
Before hiding the face under makeup,
And trying to fit your body in a dress smaller,
Before shutting them in red or pink, let the lips say
"You're beautiful".
And even when it sounds like a lie, say it.
Be it a whim, a responsibility, a grief or an illness,
There must have been some reason for your form...
But what can be more beautiful than this?
What can be more beautiful than this; that this
form of you, took care of the soul above outer
beauty.

So once again, absorb this truth, and tell yourself
"You are beautiful".


-        PoeTiK

# Penning My Story

Can someone pen
down my story?
The paths I tread
along my journey;
Can someone
write, the screams
suppressed by
these walls,
The tears behind
the veil,
And the reason for my silence.
The death of my patience,
And the never-ending pain,
The prolonged uneasiness.
Or will someone just keep describing,
My dark-hued locks, which camouflage the
darkest stories,
Or about my deep brown eyes, which try to
express what the lips don't,
Or just about the beauty that is fading away.
Can someone pen down my story?


-        PoeTiK

# Don't love me, but..

I was lost at the
moment I saw
you.
In a way I had
surrendered to
you. 
Didn't know if
you saw me too,
But I don't even want your attention.
The love I have for you in my heart is not an
attachment,
Just a feeling I want to own all my life.
I don't want you to want me too,
Even if you ever feel like it, just a glance will do
enough,
For me to live this life.
I understand, love is not an exchange,
The way I feel for you, not necessary that you
should feel the same.
What I wish for is different, while your
perspective of looking at things will be different.
I don't want to change you at all, because I love
you for what you are.
But a request, may I?
Don't love me, but don't hate me either.

Although it means my existence is zilch, your presence means everything to me.


-       PoeTiK

# Do You Realize???

I want to keep
writing those lines,
That keep reaching
the depths of your
heart.
Every moment, all
the time,
The lines that keep
me reminding of
you.
My words in my
poetry, keep
mentioning you, over and over again.
Do you realize, there is still someone?
Someone who loves you till today, just the way
it was yesterday.

-      PoeTiK

# Failed Deal

The love I had, I
could never
express.
We spent hours
together,

The terms we
had, were
acceptable to each other,
But never reached an agreement,
Alas! This togetherness never landed in
affection.
Uncertain how to measure the depth of this
relationship,
This confused state of mind never climbed the
summit of Love.
This deal of heart never made it to business.


-       PoeTiK

# Complete The Incomplete

One day at a crossing,
Two incompletes
collided with each
other.
He was just running
away from something,
Solving this puzzle was also part of his race.
She also was coming from somewhere else,
Searching for her lost self in hundreds of
questions.
The two incompletes met and completed each
other.
She taught her to stay calm, and he simplified
for her the answers she was looking for.
They spent the evenings together and saw the
moon in each other's arms.
He kept talking, she kept listening,
Her silence used to answer all his questions.
Then one day, both took new paths for
themselves...
After some time apart, they felt the
incompleteness again,
Now they are wandering again in search of
completing this feeling of incompleteness.

-       PoeTiK